A LIFE UNEXPECTED

The Linda Cristal Story

LINDA CRISTAL AND JORDAN WEXLER

Balboa Press books may be ordered through booksellers or by contacting:

Balboa Press
A Division of Hay House
1663 Liberty Drive
Bloomington, IN 47403
www.balboapress.com
1 (877) 407-4847

ISBN: 978-1-9822-2016-7 (sc)
ISBN: 978-1-9822-2017-4 (e)

Library of Congress Control Number: 2019900594

Print information available on the last page.

Balboa Press rev. date: 02/12/2019

BALBOA.
PRESS
A DIVISION OF HAY HOUSE

Contents

I dedicate this book to my sons,
Jordan and Gregory.

Once upon a time, there were three musketeers,
Then there were two, and then one.

I will soon enter your past.
Let's celebrate the occasion!

When I am on "the other side,"
I know it will be unimaginably beautiful there.

And there, we will be three again!
We will fly between all celestial bodies,
straight to paradise!

Dear readers,

Here are a few short stories of my travels in the film lands of the world: from South America to Europe and on. A lot of laughs sprinkled with salty tears for good measure.

I'd like to tell you about the day I fell in love with myself. I know it sounds presumptuous, but the fact is, I did.

Today is my birthday. I am 86 years old and have been a movie star since I was thirteen.

At this moment, I am sitting in my office trying to write a book and wondering if it is too late to start. Well…this is food for thought....

I have wandering eyes; they run away like unfaithful lovers, looking at my collection of awards and photos with exciting actors I have worked with from around the world.

I lean back in my reclining chair and trap my eyes by closing them. No more escapades. I need to concentrate....

Chapter 1

LINDA THE GRASSHOPPER

Lifting my feet onto the ottoman, I reminisce. I met with presidents from different countries, I have flown to the edge of the atmosphere, I have been awarded multiple Golden Globes, Emmys, and international awards for acting; not bad for girl who grew up in poverty, and who lost her parents the age of thirteen. But I am getting ahead of myself.

As you can imagine, I experienced many obstacles growing up. But there has always been a pattern. Whenever life threw me an impossible situation, I always made it possible. I embraced it without hesitation.

You see, poverty was just one of the many hurdles I would face. But we weren't always poor. In fact, until I was five, we had money. Not a lot, but more than most.

At the time there was five of us, my father, mother brothers Antonito and Miguel and myself. We lived in a town called Mataderos, a suburb of Buenos Aires named for the cities main occupation of slaughtering cattle, amongst other things.

My father was very successful and owned a magazine. Upon hearing of its success, the local mafia wanted a piece of it. My father, who worked very hard building it, refused.

A short time later, I was playing in the street with my friends, one of whom looked very much like me and in fact had the same first name, Martita. While we were playing, my mother called me in for lunch, so I ran into the house.

Two or three days later, my father came home agitated and I saw he had a newspaper in his pocket. He called my mother and I could see on the newspaper a picture of a pizza oven and next to it, the photograph of a little girl, who looked remarkably like me.

My father said, "They baked her like a piece of bread."

My mother said, "Who?"

And he responded, "Martita, the neighbor's daughter…"

My eyes opened wide in horror.

He turned to her, trying to speak under his breath, "You know why this happened, right? The mafia thought they grabbed our girl…."

With that my mother gasped, "We have to run away."

My father walked over to the window. Noticing two black cars driving by repeatedly, he responded, "By now they must know they got the wrong girl."

My mom, looking scared, responded, "What are we going to do? We need to move far away…fast…like to Europe."

"No," my father said, "that is what they would expect. We will wait till nighttime and escape across the river to Montevideo in Uruguay. We can't take anything but what we can carry ourselves, so as not to alert them."

"What about money? What about your business? How will we eat?"

And just like that, we went from having money to living in a dungeon in Montevideo. My life changed overnight. No luxuries, no friends, and no hope.

I remember the place where we lived very well. It was a small portion of a square block that once had been the house of the viceroy from Spain. Later on, it had become an asylum, and now it was a tenement house for the poor. There were no other children in the place. So I used to walk around, up and down, fantasizing.

My mother's dream was to be on the stage. Even though she had neglected me since the day I was born, I had feelings for her that I couldn't explain. I loved her and hated her. While I couldn't understand my dilemma, I had a strange attachment to her.

Much later in life I would come to learn that we always want what we don't have.

Why can't a rose open in its entire splendor and go back to being a bud again? I don't know, but this rose—me—will!

Dear reader, let's dream together. I am sure at one time or another in your life something happened that will make you identify with me. Who was it that said, "Que será, será?"

The fact is, I adored my mother. Like a little ember in the forest, my love for her grew and grew until it became a bonfire.

I will be on stage for her! I will be recognized all around the world for her! I will learn languages and do films and I know somewhere up there, she will look down upon me and smile, a smile that I never saw when she was alive.

But for now, I was only five years old, with nothing to do but explore the dungeon and the surrounding areas.

My father spent most of his time in the cellar building devices to display clothes, which he could sell to stores—while my mother helped him, or sat for long periods of time, singing to entertain him.

I began to walk the two blocks that separated us from the harbor where the big ships from around the world arrived. One of the ships had a sign that said USA and there were sailors talking next to it.

I approached them with my hand stuck out, and one of them put a coin in it. I looked at it and put it in my other hand, and extended my hand out again.

He laughed and said, "Money, huh?"

I said, "Money…money…"

And he put another coin in it.

The sailor laughed and said, "Look. Here, put your two hands together and I will give you a lot of little coins." And he filled my hands with coins.

With that, I smiled and then ran home to my parents, thinking now I could support them.

Time goes by, and so did the obstacles.

May the time I was about 8, my father was able to sell some of his metal articles for store windows, which allowed us to move from the basement to the first floor of the dungeon.

My favorite brother, Antonito, was working as a designer in a store. But he began to lose weight rapidly and couldn't work anymore.

In the space we occupied there were two rooms: Antonito slept in the one with the balcony, and my parents and I slept in the other one.

One day there was a hush in the place, and my parents would not let me go in to see my brother. I peeked in anyway, and my brother, seeing me, waved me away.

What I saw petrified me. He was as thin as a skeleton, and I didn't know what to make of it. Two days later I was sent away to live with one of my mother's women friends, and when I came back there was no more Antonito—and no explanations.

Dear readers, to lose a loved one in a week is painful beyond description, but tragic events were not finished with me yet.…

One night, about 5 years later, I was sleeping in my brother's old room when I heard my father's voice coming from the kitchen area, saying "Oh my God… Oh my God."

My mother had passed away. I think it was a result of a diabetic attack, as we had no money to buy insulin.

My father, who loved her very much, opened the gas valve, laid next to her, and died as well.

The next morning, when I discovered what happened, I told my brother, who was hard to awake do to his drunkenness. I told him that something was wrong and that our parents were not in their bed.

He stumbled into the hall that led to the kitchen, and looking through the glass, he saw our parents lying dead on a blanket.

He turned to me and said, "Martita, our parents are dead and I have to go to work. You need to stay with them for the 'Velada.'" When I return, I will handle everything.

The Velada was a ritual that after death, in which bodies were exposed to the family for a period of about 12 hours.

This is an image that as long as I live, I will never be able to erase from my mind. My father eyes closed, not in the relaxing look of sleep, but in a strange closed-ness that tells you they will never be open again.

After 12 hours, I walked the two blocks to the harbor, looked at the ships, and decided that I was leaving in one of them. I noticed people getting on the boat, stood next to a family with many children, and walked onto the ship with them. It was so busy, nobody noticed me.

Then I climbed into a lifeboat and pulled the tarp over the top, hiding myself. Where the ship went was not my concern, I just wanted to get away.

There was an anger in me that grew like a bonfire. A mixture of the love I had for my parents, and the hate because they didn't say goodbye. While I loved my brother, he had a life and a job and he could take care or himself.

As for me, I channeled my anger into a drive to make it for them. What they didn't have in life, I would make it for myself in their memory.

So, there I was in the boat. In the evenings, I would get out, and eat and drink with the rest of the passengers. When it was time to sleep, I would go back to my little lifeboat.

One early morning, a loud siren rang and I noticed we were arriving somewhere. A banner said MÉXICO. Getting off the boat, I grabbed a movie magazine that someone had dropped, and began to read it as we were disembarking.

I said to myself, *That's it! I will search in movie magazines, and learn to imitate successful people. I will add to that some paprika, a little pepper, thyme, and whatever else is handy, and voilà—the new Linda Cristal will be created.*

I found out that some of the stories were not acceptable to me and others were more manageable. I just had to be selective, inventive, and daring.

In the magazine I read, there was a very famous actor/mime mentioned. His name was Cantinflas. I had seen him in magazines and posters, wearing his pants way below his belly button and a tank top that didn't even come close to reaching his pants. He wore a colorful little handkerchief around his neck, and an old hat that had seen better days. There was a quizzical look in his eyes that I will never forget.

A memory came to me: my brother Antonito imitating Charlie Chaplin, a stick in his hand, walking back and forth—which made me laugh and laugh when I was five years old. It was his way of wiping away my tears when my mother was cruel to me.

But Cantinflas was a millionaire—and, reportedly, unusually generous. The poor stood around his block every year to receive money for their Christmas. A man like that would for sure help me when I told him my story.

I said to myself, *That's the answer right there. All I have to do is get to him.*

I opened up the telephone book, looked under Cantinflas Productions, and found his address on Reforma Avenue, in Mexico City.

Easy—I would become a "grasshopper" and jump my way toward him. Why waste time thinking? Moments later, I was on my way.

When I arrived to his office, I rang the bell and a man answered, "Yes, Can I help you?"

I hesitated and then quickly responded, I am here to see Mr. Cantinflas, please tell him Ms. Cristal is here.

Moments later, I was facing a gentleman dressed in a very elegant suit, with exquisite manners, "Please sit down, Mrs. Cristal."

I did, sitting at the edge of the chair, holding my knees together with my hands so they wouldn't shake.

I cleared my throat and said, "How shall I address you, Mr. Moreno?"

He giggled and sat down himself. "No, Linda, call me Mario or whatever you're comfortable with. Cantinflas, if you like."

"Well, here it is," I said and sighed, "I desperately need to work. The union won't allow me to work because I am Argentinean and never acted in my country. They also say I am too white, my accent doesn't sound Mexican, and my features are not Mexican."

He giggled. "But, Linda, that makes you unique. You're one of a kind."

My eyes looked up to him, filled with hope and yet incredulous. "You mean like a Frankenstein?"

He looked at me and began to laugh. I joined him, laughing too, and wiping away tears of happiness.

Chapter 2

LINDA THE BUTTERFLY

After tossing and turning in bed half the night, I finally fell asleep. I dreamed I was a butterfly. I was flying from flowers to fountains when a sudden gust of wind pushed me strongly.

I woke up, my heart pounding, and realized it was only a dream. Turning over, I searched for Mr. Sleep. I fell asleep again, only to find myself trapped in the same dream, but with my wings blown off. I was now a mere brown worm, crawling on the ground, screaming, "Mama! Mama!"

There was no answer.

"Do you love me?"

No answer again.

"Did you ever love me when I was little?" My own voice woke me up.

I sat up slowly, thinking, *Was I like that butterfly?*

What is a butterfly but a little worm crowned by two gorgeous multicolored wings, painted by the greatest painter ever—Mother Nature.

I sat at the edge of my bed. The sun was beginning to reveal the colors on the walls around me.

Yes, it's time for another venture. Dear reader, do you want to fly with me?

Filled with the confidence of Cantinflas, his words still ringing in my ears, I went to meet a man he suggested I speak with.

As I approached a building on Avenida Reforma, I noticed the brown sign on the right, which read PEDRO CALDERON PRODUCTIONS. I was disappointed to see that the office would not open for half an hour.

I looked up at the building. It was a two-story colonial building, hugged by another building of the same style. It brought to mind a line of suspects, their mugs being photographed in profile, before being thrown in the can.

I leaned against the wall again and gave my imagination the reins. I love to philosophize when I have time.

The fidelity of man came to mind. Why does this creature need more than one woman to satisfy his libido? This applies to any man, from a gardener to the president of a country. Is nature involved in his decision? As the French say, "Vive la différence."

I was about to encounter one of the opposite sex…my knight in shining armor, Pedro Calderon.

I walked toward the street, looked at the building again, and saw the thinnest muslin curtains I had ever seen. They were flowing in and out, like a welcoming gesture. Very inviting… Was this a come-on? But what were the intentions behind it?

Dear reader, more to come! Don't turn the page. I don't mind confessing that I am dying to know more myself!

When the secretary opened the door to his office, a rush of air conditioning entered the room with me. The curtains seemed to escape from the balcony, as if they were convicts running from the law.

This is for my female readers: Do you believe in signs? I do. At that moment, I should have turned my back and ran away, as quick as a horse at the derby. But I didn't.

As I walked in, I covered my eyes to avoid the strong sunlight. Noticing that, Pedro proceeded to shut the windows.

"Is that better?" he asked.

I replied, "Yes, thank you."

Coming around the desk, he said, "At this time of the morning, the air is still fresh, so I like to keep the windows open." He shook my hand.

He was the dream come true of any young woman in the world.

I noticed he was looking me up and down, like he was undressing me with his eyes. At the touch of his hand, I felt something I had never felt before: it was like magic. Do you know what I mean? I shivered.

Pedro continued, "Do you like rock 'n' roll?"

Dear readers, did I tell you about the cupid I have sitting on my left shoulder? Well, he loves risk. He always tells me, "Linda, if you don't risk, you don't win. You have to take a chance. "

My eyes rushed to meet Pedro's. He was smiling.

"Oh…oh…of course… I probably would if I heard more of it."

There was a knock at the door and the male secretary opened it just a few inches, murmuring, "Pedro, there's a storm coming—driving a Porsche."

The stardust falling gently over Pedro Calderon and I seemed to stop in midair. What did the man mean—a storm driving a Porsche?

Pedro regained his position behind the desk and, sitting down, placed both hands on the desk in front of him as if he were in a plane that was about to crash.

The office door opened with such vigor, a painting fell.

"Oye, chico!" She spoke like a cyclone, not stopping to breathe at all. She was so focused on Pedro, she didn't even see me.

The secretary extended his hand to me, motioning me out of the room. He raised his finger to his lips saying, "Shh," and murmured, "Mr. Calderon will be in touch with you, where can we reach you?"

While walking to the streetcar, I sighed and thought to myself, " ahh…what a man."

Finally I exhaled and got on the streetcar.

A week later, Pedro called and said, "Linda?"

"Pedro?"

"I arranged for Fidel to pick you up and drive you to the airport. I will meet you at my house in Acapulco this afternoon."

What a surprise, I thought to myself, but then, I love surprises.

"I will be ready."

The beauty of the bay was beyond anything I had ever seen. It was like the hand of God extending out over the rocky mountains, where the mansion sat at the tips of God's fingers.

The house was actually a palace, overlooking the whole bay of Acapulco.

Upon my arrival, a bunch of servants ran to meet me, picking up my luggage, taking off my coat, and showing me the way to a bedroom.

One of them had a tall drink on a silver platter, with a slice of pineapple on the side and a long straw sticking out. It looked delicious.

I followed them to an elegant bedroom with a high ceiling. On the night table next to the bed, there was a picture of the Mulata cyclone.

Many emotions rushed me. I had butterflies in my stomach. Why? And why did those butterflies have black wings? Was this a premonition?

When I was left alone in the room, and the door was closed, I laid back on the bed and closed my eyes to rest, listening to the sea in the distance.

I must have dozed off. When I woke up it was morning, and there was no sign of Pedro.

I waited day after day, thinking that something must have detained him and that he would be there the following day without a doubt. But a whole week went by, and still no Pedro.

When Fidel saw my nervous squirming, he said maybe we should go back into town, so you can speak to him.

Back at the Reforma hotel, where I was staying, the phone rang. The music from the intercom was filtering a song by Johnny Mathis: *"Smile if your heart is aching, smile even though it's breaking."*

Sitting at the edge of the bed, feeling sorry for myself, I jumped as if the phone was a cobra ready to bite. My nerves were on edge.

I picked it up with trembling fingers. It was the concierge. "Ms. Cristal, there is a gentlemen by the name of Fidel, he has a delivery for you."

I dug into my heart, trying to understand what I felt. Was it happiness? Anger? Both? All I knew was that there were tears fighting to burst out of my eyes, but I wasn't going to cry. I was going to hold them back.

After taking a deep breath, I told the concierge, "Could you please have someone bring the package to me? Thank you."

When he handed me the little pastry bag, I looked at it with curiosity. What in the heck…? I looked into the bag. There was a three-strand Cartier bracelet with a matching ring. I had seen that set at Cartier's window at the corner of the hotel.

I picked up the bracelet to admire the perfection of the square diamonds that studded the bracelet and ring. Looking for an answer, I looked in the bag again and saw a card, which simply read,

"Dinner tonight, you and I?"

And so, time went by.…

Whenever Pedro didn't show, he sent his replacement: another little bag.

Chapter 3

PEDRO CALDERON

Even if rock 'n' roll wasn't my cup of tea, I learned to enjoy it.

I would go back to my hotel and practice dancing in front of the mirror with enthusiasm, and then laugh at myself, giggling and falling back on the bed exhausted. It was fun.

The next day, I sat in my chair on the movie set and stretched my legs in front of me, closing my eyes for a moment. Suddenly I had the feeling that someone was sitting next to me.

I heard his voice before I turned my head. It was Pedro. He said, "Remember what Fidel told you when we first met in my office, about the storm driving a Porsche?"

I looked at him and after a moment I said, "Yes. I do."

He continued, "The storm was Amelita." He went on, "Calderon Productions owns a satellite company. It is a long story, I won't go into it now.

"On one of my trips, I went to Havana. Walking around, taking in the sights, I saw a nightclub. The sound of drums was loud and tickled my curiosity, so

I went in.

"It was a small café, smelling strongly of drunk sailors, bongo music, people whistling and cheering the dancer on.

"She was a beautiful *mulata* and was being teasingly provocative to the sailors, who cheered her on. I invited her to my table and she said her name was Amelita Vargas."

I continued to listen to Pedro, when all of a sudden the lights went on and the entire set became as clear as day. Pedro jumped up like a jack in the box and walked toward the entrance of the set.

As he did, I looked at him. His square shoulders ended in very slender hips, and I noticed the most attractive pair of muscly buttocks ever.

Pedro had the body of an athlete. But—was his mind also an athlete that was going to make me walk the tightrope? And if I got to the other side, would I find smiles or tears on my face?

The filming went on. In the evenings, the three of us went to dinner, Pedro, Fidel, and I. Pedro and I were never together alone.

Once, when Fidel and I were alone, he said, "Linda, did Pedro tell you about Amelita Vargas?" I answered yes.

"Let me give you a one-liner," he said. "Amelita is a very lucrative savage."

"Why a savage?" I asked, not understanding what he meant.

"With her, Pedro has to accept her demands, no questions asked. There are many things involved…bad things. She shoots from the hip and asks questions later. She said if she saw Pedro with another woman, she would shoot the woman on sight."

I listened in amazement.

As time went by, Fidel's words rang in my ears. All I could think was that Pedro was carrying a ball and chain tied to his ankle, engraved: OWNED BY AMELITA VARGAS.

I wish I had a cupid on my shoulder that told me what to do. When my heart tells me to follow love, my cupid would say, "Don't be stupid."

Dear reader: Did you ever find yourself at such a fork in the road? What would you have done?

The phone rang. It was Pedro.

"Linda."

"Yes."

"Time to do the locations in Acapulco." I heard a hint of a giggle in his voice, which told me that this time we were going together, and I would remain there until the end of the film.

"Happy?"

"Absolutely," I replied.

Acapulco was beautiful. We often went to La Perla, a restaurant at the El Mirador hotel. On one side was a rocky mountain, where the divers stood, waiting to jump in the water when the powerful waves rushed in, crowned by white foam.

On the other side, there was night-blooming jasmine cascading over the rocks. In between, there was another level, with small tables arranged with chairs.

In the middle, there was an area to dance, big enough for twelve couples or so. I had never seen anything so romantic. I had heard that famous singers such as Frank Sinatra and Tom Jones, and local singers such as Trio Los Ponchos and Trio Los Caballeros, would perform regularly.

I was, as always, seated between Fidel and Pedro, longing to be dancing with Pedro—but no dice.

I closed my eyes for a moment and saw myself on the dance floor, my arms reaching around his neck, my lips touching his cheek, my body encrusted against him.

Pedro's voice brought me out of my reverie. I looked up at him.

"Are you alright?"

Dear reader, let's face it. Reveries will never be realities.

Let me tell you what happened in the bedroom of Pedro's palace. We were finally alone together. I looked at him with longing, desire.…

He sat at the edge of the bed, facing me. There was a sad smile on his lips, and he said, "Let me explain. Amelita…"

That dear cupid must have had an ice bucket in his hands, because it was as if he had dumped it on the top of my head.

I said, "Oh no, there is nothing to explain…there is no reason to explain anything. If I hadn't been such a stupid dreamer, this wouldn't have happened. I know it all and I understand. Let's call this episode in our lives a figment of my imagination and let's part."

Before he could say a word, I walked out of the room, wishing I had wings to quickly fly away.

When I got back to my apartment, I called downstairs and told them to bring up the container that I had placed there for safety. Then I called a security guard from the jewelry store and asked him to come upstairs. I placed the box in his hands and said, "Please return this personally to Mr. Pedro Calderon on Avenida Reforma."

I began to pack my luggage, and after a while the phone rang. The concierge downstairs said, "The guard is back and he wants to talk to you."

I opened the door. "I did as you told me, ma'am, but the person who answered said I had the wrong address. There was no person by that name." The guard put the package back in my hands.

When the guard left, I sighed. Well, they say life is made of moments and memories. I had great moments with Pedro and I always wanted to wear beautiful jewelry, so why fight God's will.

Que será, será…

Chapter 4

HOWARD HUGHES

Landing at Los Angeles International airport, I was surprised not to see reporters waiting for my arrival, especially since I had completed a few movies. I was sure the studio would have notified them.

Someone touched me on my shoulder. "Excuse me, you are Linda Cristal, aren't you?"

I turned around to a cartoon-like face with bulging eyes.

Extending his hand, he said, "My name is Carl Kruger. I am with United Artists productions. May I take a picture of you? I want to show it to the head of the studio. You are gorgeous!"

I was surprised. I didn't know what to make of his proposal.

"Let me explain—I want you to become my discovery. Like Lana Turner, Rita Hayworth, you will be up there in shining letters in all the theaters in Hollywood. United Artists is one of the most important studios in Hollywood."

I kept staring at him and, realizing I had to answer the man, I said, "Well… as a matter of fact—"

He interrupted me. "It will be a week at the most. I will rent an apartment for you across the street from my house, where I live with my wife in the flats of Beverly Hills."

Dear reader, I wondered if it was déjà vu or luck knocking on my door. I wasn't going to take a chance, since luck doesn't always knock twice.

The next morning at 8 a.m., the phone rang. Lifting my head, I wished the phone hadn't rung. I wanted to sleep some more. I picked it up.

"Yes? Hello?"

A vigorous voice answered, "Wake up sleeping beauty, we hit the jackpot. Have you heard of Howard Hughes?"

I thought for a moment. Howard…Hughes? No.

"Well, I'll tell you. Dress yourself for the occasion. Dress as if you're going to receive your first Oscar. I will pick you up in one hour."

Trying to make heads and tails of the command, I walked lazily to the shower.

More alert after my shower, I applied lipstick very carefully, drew a brush through my long black hair, got dressed, and looked out the window. A car was waiting outside and Carl was leaning on it.

I got in his shiny Mercedes and away we went.

Soon after, we stopped in front of a two-story building on Sunset Boulevard. On the facade, I read WALTER CAIN, PHOTOGRAPHER.

Carl parked the car in front and opened the door for me. We went up a flight of stairs and Carl introduced me, "Linda Cristal…Walter Cain."

He said, "Charmed. This way, please."

Stepping out into the terrace, I looked around for the important man, but there was no one there. On the right was a geranium, sitting on the edge of the terrace, overhanging with sadness due to its lack of water. It was a hot summer day and the sun was beating mercilessly on the cement floor of the terrace.

"If Ms. Cristal would like to sit in this chair, Mr. Hughes would like to interview her for an hour."

I said, "It's very hot today, may I sit in the shade while I wait?

"No, you need to sit in that chair and don't move. Mr. Hughes is very precise. He wants enough light on you to see you clearly."

This situation was surreal, but I had to go by what Kruger said.

Time passed. I felt a drop of perspiration running down between my breasts. I began to fan myself with my hand and looked around for a spot of shade where I could wait.

Beginning to get bored, I stood up and walked to the veranda, looking down onto the street, where the cars drove up and down.

An old Ford stopped and parked illegally in front of the building.

The man who stepped out was handsome and very tall, perhaps six-foot-six. He came into the building and soon I heard Kruger saying, "Good morning, Mr. Hughes, my client is on the terrace." There was no answer.

I immediately sat in the designated chair.

He was dressed in a white T-shirt and jacket; no tie. He was wearing loafers with no socks. There was no expression on his face. He reminded me of Pinocchio, when he's only a puppet.

He looked at me, and very calmly walked to his chair and sat down. I had been told that I was not to talk to Hughes unless he talked to me first. So, I didn't.…

Time passed very slowly. As far as I was concerned, it felt like ten hours had passed. All he did was sit motionless and stare at me. This definitely was going to be torture, but I would show him I could take it.

At times he would furlough his brow, and other times he would seem to be calculating. Suddenly, after about an hour, he just stood up and walked out.

I thought to myself, "What a fucking…"

Carl drove me back to my apartment and invited me to dinner at his house that night.

He said, "We will expect you at seven o'clock, okay, honey? Cheer up, I think we won the lottery."

When I arrived at his house for dinner, his wife opened the door. She was a very unattractive little woman, with a nose belonging to a bad boxer. The house was very unpretentious.

After dinner we had coffee in the den. She kept looking at her shoes and crossing her legs and I wondered if she wanted me to notice them. So I said, "I love your shoes."

I excused myself to go to the powder room, but left the door ajar. While I was washing my hands, I heard her say, "But she's a Latino, for God's sake, let her do my dishes!"

To which Carl said, "Shh...she is a movie star and she is going to be our pot of gold.... Now don't be stupid."

A couple of days went by. Then, Carl called me on the phone and said, "It seems that it didn't work out, babe. I think you would do better back in Mexico."

I wondered what had happened; however, I was too proud to ask.

I said, "Of course, no problem. Let me call you back."

I turned around, hugged the pillow, and cried into it.

I later found out that Howard Hughes did make an offer the day after we met: a million dollars for a 7 year movie contract. Greedy Carl countered, asking for ten million. When he didn't receive a response, he called, only to find out from his secretary that Mr. Hughes did not make counter-offers and the deal was dead.

But at the time, I didn't know this, so I simply said to myself, "C'mon, Linda, you're not going to give up, it's not in your nature." So I went to sleep, thinking of what to do.

The next morning, waking up, it was like someone touched me on the shoulder and advised me to go see Walter Cain. I wasn't sure if it was part of my dream, or what. I stretched, sat at the edge of my bed, and finally resolved to see Cain.

I rang for a taxi, arrived at his place on Sunset Boulevard, and rang the bell.

Someone answered. "Oh yes, Ms. Cristal, I'll tell Mr. Cain you're here."

He was sitting in his living room and didn't get up, so I approached his chair. He placed his right hand on my hip bone. I found the gesture inappropriate, but I ignored it, hoping he could help me.

Cain said, "You would make a perfect model, Linda, you're not only gorgeous but so slender."

I relayed what had happened between Carl and Howard Hughes.

"Perfect," he said. "Let him send you to Mexico and I will bring you back."

I believed him. I went back to my apartment, packed, and went to Mexico. Three weeks went by and not a word from Cain.

"Alright, Walter Cain, you were a sack of shit after all."

Chapter 5

DANA ANDREWS

But as luck would have it, none other than Carl Kruger called. He was now producing a movie starring Dana Andrews called *Comanche,* which would be shot in Durango, Mexico and he thought I would be perfect for the leading female role.

I spent the night dreaming up possibilities. What would he look like, this Dana Andrews? Was Durango primitive? Obviously it was a big production, because the cast was excellent. I closed my eyes and said, "What am I doing trying to guess what I don't know? Instead I should get some sleep, to look good in the morning."

As I descended from the small plane, a wave of hot air caressed my face. There was a chauffeur waiting and he opened the door to the limousine. I got in. Leaning back and closing my eyes, I wondered how long the ride would be.

I asked the chauffeur, "Does it get any hotter here?"

"Oh," he laughed, "it gets plenty hot, my lady, but you'll get used to it."

Upon arriving, the phone rang and it was Mr. Kruger. "Linda, the cast and crew have dinner every night on the terrace. Why don't you join us when you're ready?"

"I would be delighted."

On the terrace there was a round table with six people around it. Two of them stood up: Kruger, and an athletic man who could have been an Olympian.

"Meet Dana Andrews, Linda. Dana, this is Linda Cristal."

We shook hands. Dana pulled out a chair for me, next to his. There was a pile of vintage records and an old Victrola record player on the table.

He began to eat and, reaching for his goblet, turned it upside down.

"Would you like some wine?"

"No, thank you, I need to memorize a few pages tonight," I said.

He placed a record on the machine, wound it up, and the song began to play: *"Don't throw bouquets at me, don't please my folks too much, don't laugh at my jokes too much, people will say we are in love..."*

I giggled, "I love that music. It's from the '60s, right?"

"Yes," Dana said. "I tell you what, why don't I bring my Victrola on location, and I will play for you all these lovely songs?"

I answered, "What a marvelous idea…thank you."

Morning came too soon, and I hurried to take a shower, wash my face, and get ready for probably an hour of makeup and hair.

The night before, Kruger had left me a script, and he'd underlined the scene we were going to film first thing in the morning. I was playing an Indian girl that had been captured by the Comanche Indians.

I went to my dressing room and there, waiting, was Ginnie, my dresser, holding a suede Indian dress for me to wear.

"Good morning," I said. "Suede? That's going to be hot."

She said, "Not too bad." She giggled and I looked up in surprise. "Listen, dear, it gets much worse under the *brutos*—you know, the light reflectors."

I giggled back. "How is the makeup man going to keep the makeup on my face before it melts down my chin?" *I guess Ginny and I are going to be good friends,* I thought.

Walking out of my dressing room, I went out onto the set. There were teepees and extras walking around them. Some had Kleenex around their necks to prevent the makeup from damaging their costumes.

Some others, who were less important, were just talking to each other and laughing. They all had a long feather sticking out from the back of their heads, held by a vincha, A ribbon that ran across their foreheads to hold a feather in the back.

There were two teepees. One for the long shots, and the other for the interior shots. Inside it, Dana lay on a blanket, waiting for me to rehearse.

Lifting the flap that covered the entrance, I said, "Good morning, I'm sorry I took so long."

"Don't worry, Linda," he said. "It's cool in here."

Shooting the interiors took five or six days. There we were, Dana and I, looking into each other's eyes. No more than a breath away.

The reality that the words implied began to turn more and more personal. The characters slowly disappeared, leaving just Dana and I.

One day we were rehearsing lines alone, and since it was so hot outside, Dana said, "Let's lower the flap and keep the air conditioning in."

My head was on his chest, as the scene required.

To my female friends reading this, you will understand what happened.…

My eyelids became heavy and closed, my stupid hand crawled up around the back of his neck, and I kissed him right on the mouth. It wasn't a hello kiss or a goodbye kiss, it was the sexiest kiss I had ever given in my whole life.

I pulled away, took a deep breath, and thought, I could tell him it's April Fool's Day. But it's not April.

That evening, I didn't go up to the terrace for dinner. I wasn't able to face him. I was too embarrassed. I had to stop this insane attraction I had for Dana. The situation had "emotional disaster" written all over it.

Still, I wanted to crash myself against Dana's body, as if I were the shuttle rushing back to Earth.

The director had me lie on my back, with a blanket rolled under my neck so the eye camera could focus on my eyes.

The dialogue started. Kreuger had explained to me that I needed to speak in broken English. I began to speak, trying to fulfill his direction.

A voice interrupted us: "Cut! Linda, a little more accent. And show more fear…. Remember, you're shaking and you've been captured by the Indians. We don't want to tell the public yet, but Dana is your savior."

I answered, "Right… I didn't have much time to read the whole script, you said one scene."

"Oh, don't worry. We are only filming this one scene today, but it has to be right."

So, the day went by and I found out that I didn't mind any of it, as long as I was in Dana's arms.

Weeks passed. The film came to an end and I had a heavy heart. Reality had taken over, and the emotions that had taken over me should have died with the character.

We all met at the airport to catch the flight to Los Angeles. I looked up at Dana with tears in my eyes.

He walked up to me and murmured, "Linda, this is for the best." He put his hands on my shoulders and said in a low voice, "Did you ever have a secret you didn't want anyone to know?"

I answered with a sob, "Yes."

He continued, "I do too." He looked at me with a mixture of longing and sadness. "But I will remember you and our moments together for the rest of my life."

Someone approached me. It was the camera operator, who put his hand on mine and said, "I knew this was going to happen to you. It happens to many actresses with their co-stars. For a few weeks, sometimes months, all they see from morning to night is the one actor they are working with. The rest of their family stops existing. In many cases, when the end comes, they are unable to disengage and go back to their lives and be happy.

"How could you expect not to fall in love with him? Look, go to the ladies room, wash your face, and come back. I am an old man and have seen them come and go for many years. I think you have the quality of a star and will go a long way, so you better save some tears, girl…or you're going to run out."

I couldn't help myself—I hugged him. I boarded the plane thinking this was going to be the most important lesson of my life.

I heard the voice of the flight attendant: "Fasten your seatbelts." After the plane took off, I just sat there, my eyes closed. I remembered that someone in the crew had told me that Dana drank. Never while filming, but the moment a picture finished he hit the bottle like there was no tomorrow.

It was hard to believe—but was that the secret he mentioned? Of course! That was it!

Chapter 6

LEON LANCE

After *Comanche* ended, I flew back to Hollywood and began flipping the pages in the telephone book, stopping at actors' agencies. I saw a two-inch ad from the William Morris agency, who handled the biggest stars in Hollywood. Next to it, there was a very small space, with the name Leon Lance agency. There was something about Leon Lance's name that seemed to reach out to me.

On an impulse, I picked up the phone and dialed his number.

"Mr. Lance? My name is Linda Cristal, and I am looking for an agent."

Leon was one of a kind. Our first interview was at United Artists. Leon came to pick me up in a battered old car. There was a baguette and a bunch of pencils tried together with a rubber band between us.

I turned to look at him and said, "Were you shopping?"

He answered, "No, this is my ammunition."

I was taken aback by this, and for a moment I thought, *Hmm…perhaps I should have signed with William Morris.*

The facade of the UA studio gave me wings. Here I was finally. The guard was very amiable with Leon. He said, "Leon…where to today?"

"Howard Christie's office," Leon replied.

As we drove through the gate, to the left was a row of offices, surrounded by a wood veranda. We went up the wood steps to the second floor, to a door that read HOWARD CHRISTIE. After knocking, we walked in.

It was then that I noticed that Leon had the pencils with the rubber band in his hand.

The secretary looked at him and said, "Ah, Leon—how are you?"

He answered, "Hello, sunshine, I have something for you." He placed the pencils in front of her.

With a giggle, she said, "Thank you, Leon."

"By the way," Leon continued, "this is Ms. Linda Cristal."

"How do you do, Ms. Cristal?" she said, standing up. I will let Mr. Christie know you're here." She knocked at his door, opened it, and said, "Leon Lance is here."

With that, we walked in, and after shaking his hand, he asked us to sit down.

He said down too, smiling at me. "Well, Ms. Cristal, you're a very beautiful young woman."

Leaning back in his chair, he seemed to debate some thoughts in his mind. "Excuse me if I am taking a little time to think this out, but the fact is, I am tempted to consider you for a part. However, you would be miscast, as your features are very refined and your skin is porcelain-white."

Leon jumped in, "Nothing makeup wouldn't fix."

Christie said, "True…true…"

He paused and then spoke again, "We are making a film with Jack Mahoney, Gilbert Roland, and Lorne Green called *The Last of the Fast Guns.*"

Christie thought for a minute and then stood up and said, "I am a man of fast decisions. When I see something is right, I don't waste any time. Can you be ready to leave for Durango, Mexico, in the morning?"

Durango again, ugh. But aren't I always bragging that I like challenges? Well, here's a juicy one.

I smiled, extending my hand. "Thank you very much, Mr. Christie, I won't disappoint you."

In *The Last of the Fast Guns,* I played the young, pregnant wife of Jake Mahoney. While being in a movie as a fat pregnant lady was not my cup of tea, I would drink it up if in the end it would advance my career. So, cheers…

Lorne Green played my uncle and Jack Mahoney and Gilbert Roland were the rest of the main characters.

My character in the film was uncomplicated, and the dialogue was short; no memorizing was required. So my evenings were filled with boredom. There was no chemistry on the set, therefore none of the romantic games actors often play with each other when on location.

One night, my eyes roaming around the room stopped on a book that someone had forgotten on the shelf. It was entitled *On Acting.*

I opened the cover and began to read about how there were two methods of acting: One is "performing," the other one is "being." The actor who performs merely delivers dialogue. The actor who uses the method of "being" is provided not only nominations, but even Academy Awards.

So, it looks like I just have to be me, join life, and be part of it, I told myself. *Otherwise I'll be on the side of the road, seeing life pass me by.*

That must have been the reason I then accepted a part in *The Fiend Who Walked the West.*

Chapter 7

ROBERT EVANS

If it was acceptable for an actor to laugh at another actor, I would still be laughing at Robert Evans.

I had heard that the Evans brothers had a lot of money—Robert's brother owned 20th Century Fox. So he probably bought the part for Robert.

The first day of shooting, Evans went into his dressing room, which was four times the size of mine or Hugh O'Brian's. He didn't come out for two or three hours. We were wondering what was going on, because men usually require very little makeup.

I was playing Hugh's pregnant wife. I must tell you that this film was pretentious—a remake of *Kiss of Death,* once played brilliantly by Richard Widmark. He had been nominated for the Oscar.

We had an hour for lunch at the *comeseria.* After a leisurely meal, we came back to find that Evans was still in his dressing room.

Finally, the door opened and I began to scream, laughing and laughing and laughing…. I couldn't help myself, I couldn't stop if my life depended on it.

Have you ever seen *The Hunchback of Notre Dame*? The famed novel by Victor Hugo? Evans looked like an elongated hunchback of Notre Dame.

The rehearsal started. Every time we started rehearsing, I began laughing. The director would say "Cut!" once again and take me to the side.

"Linda, you have to stop this," he murmured with a partial smile. "I know what you're thinking, but even if he is overacting, you can't laugh.

He and his brother are too powerful in the industry and we won't work again."

It took every fiber of my being to control what I felt, remembering that I was an actress and should be able to deliver.

Before I close this chapter, I want to share with you a funny event with a charming old man....

While filming, I saw a very old man with a battered straw hat on his head, sitting on a rock in the sun. I couldn't help but ask him, "Why are you sitting there in the sun with all this heat?"

He responded, leaning toward me in quiet voice, "So it doesn't come out and bite me."

I thought the sun had affected him. Half giggling, I said, "That's funny...who is going to bite you?"

And he responded, in a low voice like a secret agent, "Do you want to see it, niña?"

I continued to laugh harder and said, "Yes, I want to see it."

He got up and, extending his arms as long as he could, he lifted a side of the rock. To my amazement, out ran a hairy tarantula the size of my hand, looking for a place to hide.

Chapter 8

LEW WASSERMAN

Once the movie ended, I flew back to Mexico City and looked for a place to stay. I didn't have much money, but found a modest hotel in the center of town.

I had read somewhere that Mexico was sinking and people were crossing the street in boats, just like in Venice. Well, that was true, but it certainly didn't look like Venice.

The porter sent the newspaper to me in the morning. I opened the front page and saw a big headline: UNIVERSAL PICTURES LOOKING FOR A YOUNG STAR TO REPLACE LEGENDARY STAR DELORES DEL RIO.

I looked at it twice; I couldn't believe it.

Next morning, after the five minutes it took me to get ready—I never wore makeup unless I was filming, drew a brush through my hair and was out the door.

Arriving at the studio, I got out of the taxi and went to the guard gate and said, "My name is Linda Cristal, I am coming to see….Oh dear, the name slipped my tongue.…"

The guard at the gate laughed, "You don't have to tell me, I can see by your beauty that you're an actress or a model," he said, smiling. "Go ahead, go on in."

I went in and walked straight ahead, feigning a courage I was far from feeling.

Now what? I asked myself.

Two men passed me on my right, carrying one of those benches for people waiting for the bus. They put it down and continued on their way.

How convenient, I thought, and sat. I had to do some thinking. I was at a fork in the road. But this road had five prongs.

I sighed.… I always believed that in order to be a bullfighter, you had to jump in the ring and wait for the bull to come out. When the bull comes out into the ring, one thinks quickly or runs—and I couldn't afford to run.

I leaned back; it was a hot day. I heard some voices, so I looked up. Across from me, in a second-story window of a tall building, someone that looked like Cary Grant came out with a mirror in his hand, putting shaving cream on his face.

I leaned back on the bench again. Another man came out, screaming, with a script in his hands, "I tell you, man…this doesn't work," he said, lifting the script in the air and walking right back in. As the voice became thinner and thinner, I heard him say, "You have to change this paragraph and that paragraph."

Now, on my right, I saw the most unbelievably gorgeous man I'd ever dreamed existed. Wow…who was he? He was followed by a long entourage of people trying to catch up to his long steps.…

"Just a minute, Rock, just a moment. They moved your set to hanger number four."

For a moment, he turned around to talk to them and his eyes stopped to look at me, then continued traveling.

Another man passed me by, stopped, then turned around to look back at me, and asked, "What movie are you in?"

I responded, laughing, "None at the moment."

The man said, "Have you thought of talking to Lew Wasserman?"

"Who is that?" I asked.

"He owns Universal and used to be an agent. In fact, I'm on my way to see him now. Let me introduce you."

To make a long story short, the meeting went well and I explained to Wasserman that my work permit was about to expire and I had just finished making a few motion pictures.

He agreed to extend it by giving me a contract to a film starting very soon, called *The Perfect Furlough.*

Universal must have seen potential in me, because they brought a trailer with wheels and set it amongst the others, with names I went gaga over: Rock Hudson, Cary Grant, and Tony Curtis, among others. It had a pink ribbon around it, with a little sign on the door saying LINDA CRISTAL. My jaw dropped open when I saw it and stopped breathing for a moment, and then caught my breath and inhaled.

I told myself, *Ha...I made it. Universal has big plans for me.*

On my dressing table there was an envelope. I picked it up and opened it; there was a sheet of paper with Lew Wasserman's name on it and a short message:

"You have a call at seven a.m. tomorrow morning."

After makeup and hair, I went where indicated. I opened the door. The room was full of reporters. There was a backdrop cloth at the end of the room and a mailbox in front of it.

Two of the studio people helped me to sit on top of the mailbox. My dressing lady told me to cross my legs and gave me a sign to hold in front of me, which said, LINDA CRISTAL, MAYOR OF UNIVERSAL CITY.

Lights flickered around me, blinding me. All I could hear was, "One more roll, one more roll." Another one said, "I think we got it."

When the reporters left, I was able to relax. Turning around to the ladies to my side, I said, "How can I be major of Universal City? Number one, I am not prepared to be a mayor, I am an actress. Number two, Universal is not a city."

They said, "You're wrong…. Universal is a city and you're the mayor for a year."

"That's a first," I said.

Chapter 9

COMING INSIDE

At the end of the day someone told me, "You're on call tomorrow morning for makeup and hair at seven a.m. at the auditorium. That's where the hundred-piece symphony plays the background music to all the movies."

What in the heck would they want to do with me there, unless.... I knew that Lew Wasserman was the type that tried to squeeze a lemon in as many ways as possible, to get more juice out of them. Oh God...I was a lemon.

The auditorium was huge. In the middle, there was a flight of stairs going up to a small round platform that held a music stand and fluffy earphones.

I climbed the stairs as I was told, feeling like I was going up to the guillotine to get my head chopped off, like Joan of Arc.

Up there, I felt like astronauts must feel when looking at Earth. The place was huge. I tried to keep my knees from knocking against each other. Thank God I was wearing a skirt and they couldn't tell.

The conductor tapped the baton and lifted both arms to begin the orchestra. I looked at the sheet music in front of me, not knowing what to expect.

It was a song in English, and I thought, *Good,* giggling to myself, *Good luck, Charlie.... ha! This is going to be fun.*

I opened my mouth but nothing came out. I cleared my throat, the director went *tap...tap...tap,* and the orchestra stopped.

He looked at me and said, "It's alright, my dear.... We will try it again."

He went *tap...tap...tap* again, and I began to sing in a timid voice,

"I saw you last night, and got that old feeling....

When you came inside, I got that old feeling."

At that point I pulled the fluffy headphones off and looked around. Some of the musicians had their hands over their mouths, others looked like they were going to throw up. I wondered, *Oh God, was I that bad?*

Then someone else giggled; then another and another, and so on. Suddenly there was a roar of laughter all around me and they began to applaud.

Perplexed, I began to descend from the platform, feeling flattened. The woman who had brought me there took my hand and said, "Linda, don't be discouraged. I'll tell you what you did."

By then everyone had left and, sitting next to me, she said, "You know when you sang, 'You came inside'?"

I said, sniffing, "Yes."

She said, "Do you know what that means?"

I said, "No."

"It means that you had intercourse with a man and he 'came' inside you."

I looked at her and raised my hand to my checks, laughing and crying at the same time. "Oh my God, how embarrassing!"

The next morning, someone showed me *Look* magazine. My picture was on the cover, with the headline LINDA CRISTAL, and in smaller letters SHOULD SOMEONE AT UNIVERSAL EXPLAIN TO GORGEOUS LINDA ABOUT THE BIRDS AND THE BEES?

And underneath it said, WELCOME TO HOLLYWOOD, LINDA! THIS GIRL IS GOING PLACES!

Popular columnist Walter Winchell had even posted in his column a comment regarding an outstanding up and coming star.

That movie column was the event that turned one more page in the story of my life and eventually turned the decades to come into a bucket full of laughter and tears.

Chapter 10

TONY CURTIS AND JANET LEIGH

They called me in to hair and makeup and I said, "Makeup and hair for what, more reporters?"

They answered, "No, no...to meet with Tony Curtis, star of *The Perfect Furlough*. We left the script on your dressing table and underlined what they are going to use for the test. And…Linda…. How fond are you of your long hair?"

I looked at her with curiosity, "Why?"

She came close to my ear. "Well, my dear, I am not supposed to tell you this, but it's being cut off."

I looked back at her with wide eyes, and said, very loudly, "Never!"

There was a knock on the door and, with the echo of my own voice ringing in my ears, I screamed, "Come in!"

The door opened cautiously and a pair of laughing eyes said, in a very British accent, "How do you do, Linda?"

It sounded remarkably like Cary Grant, but it most definitely was not Cary Grant. He introduced himself as Tony Curtis.

I answered jokingly, in a British accent, "Come in, please."

We both laughed as he walked in to shake my hand and sat down next to me, awkwardly close.

He chose to ignore my discomfort and, and turning to me looking into my eyes, he said, "Let's get acquainted. Let me tell you about me. I had one dream through my entire life: to wake up one morning, look in the mirror, and see Cary Grant. If there was anything in the world I wanted more than winning an Academy Award, it was to be born Cary Grant."

I said, "You're crazy, you're very handsome—why do you have to be someone else?"

"Well, perhaps you're right," he said. "Lovely to meet you and see you on the set." And he left.

Dear friends and readers, one night I couldn't sleep. When I finally did, I had a terrifying nightmare. I woke up with my nightgown stuck to my skin with perspiration, my heart running like a racehorse at the derby.

In my nightmare, the Boston Strangler had both his hands around my neck, only…he looked a lot like Tony Curtis! But not the Tony that starred in *The Perfect Furlough.*

Interestingly enough, this nightmare actually came true years later, when he played the Boston Strangler in England. The makeup department made his nose straighter and wider, and when he looked at the camera in a close-up he looked terrifying.

That was when his brilliant creativity as a dramatic performer exploded, like a bonfire worthy of an Academy Award.

This opportunity would never have been offered to him in the USA, though he was a multifaceted actor, typecast as a comedian. Something similar happened to me with the role of Cleopatra. While I was competent to play the part, I did not have the fame of Elizabeth Taylor.

I had a couple of episodes with Tony that I thought were very funny. One of them occurred when filming *The Perfect Furlough.* Tony was supposed to be kept away from the gorgeous, voluptuous Sandra Rocca, played by me.

In the scene, Tony had tied several sheets together, to climb down from his balcony to mine, while the soldiers guarded his door so he wouldn't get out. Despite them, he dropped down to my room via the window, with a bottle of champagne in the pocket of his robe.

Still hanging from the sheet, he saw me in bed. With a smile full of mischievousness, he said, "Sandra, I found you. The entire army couldn't keep me away from you."

At that moment, the cork on the champagne bottle, which was hanging at the height of his pelvis, shot off like a gun. He covered the mouth of the bottle, still smiling at me.

Another funny thing happened while filming with Janet Leigh, Tony's wife in real life. She was suspicious of Tony's philandering eye, stealing glances at me when she was turned away, and she developed a great hate for me.

One morning when shooting a scene in the back lot of the studios, the department had brought a shower on wheels, because Janet's character was going to push me into a vat of red wine.

At the moment that we were leaning over and she was supposed to push me, a little of my Scarlett O'Hara spirit broke loose and, grabbing the edge of her jacket strongly, I made sure she went in with me.

The next thing I heard, was "Cut…cut… What happened? Linda, only you were supposed to go in."

With my most innocent expression, I said, "Oh…really?"

The director sighed and said, "Linda, you're in the next scene, so go take a shower and go to the set. We'll see you there."

While I was being tended by makeup, hair stylists, and wardrobe, Janet broke onto the set, covered with red wine, and said, "This is unacceptable. I refuse to work with this wetback! I will not finish the film. See if you can find someone to replace me in the next twenty-four hours."

I got up and, with another innocent expression, which not even an angel in heaven could beat, I said, "Janet…dear… Are you upset with me?"

Chapter 11

CARY GRANT

The studio began publicity shots to promote *The Perfect Furlough.* They called Cary Grant, who was on the lot and also under contract and he met us on the back lot to do the publicity shots.

So there we were: Cary, a horse, and me. He was on one side of the horse, and I was on the other. The studio took shots like they were trying to record something for history, roll after roll of film. Some with him hugging me, some where he was looking into my eyes.

On another day, trying to tie us together so rumors would start, the studio arranged for us to attend a dinner together in Beverly Hills.

While dancing together, he pulled me closer to him than was necessary. I looked up at his eyes, looking for the answer to his bold approach, and I saw two black eyes as deep as black holes in space.

Fear took over me. My mind was racing.

I remembered that in any love affair, there was always one who loved more, and it was better to be the one who loved less. Cary would always be the one who loved more. Who would not fall madly in love with Cary Grant?

On the other hand, if I could close my eyes and give myself entirely to that love, what a journey that would be. This moment of choice would change my entire life.

Cary began to call me at home and ask me to go out to dinner, which I continued to turn down. Finally, he called and said, in his charming accent, "Linda, would you like to go to a baseball game with me?"

I responded, "Baseball… Well, I like basketball."

He said, "No, Linda, baseball is a fun game, let me show it to you, come with me."

Who could say no to Cary Grant? I couldn't.

From then on, we went to dinner parties, award events—we went everywhere together.

We continued dating, but the closer I got to him, the more he scared me. He was so famous and handsome, and I was afraid to become the one who loved more. I refused to lose control of my emotions. I learned my lesson with Pedro and Dana.

But..maybe I should have. What do you think?

Looking back, I say to myself, *Oh what a fool I was.* Unfortunately, foolishness is something you pay for in installments for the rest of your life.

Every once in a while, when I take a nap or retire for the evening, I close my eyes and Cary is there.

Once upon a time, I married a young man, who would have been considered a prince to any young woman around me. He was gentle, intelligent, well-read. And a bit dependent.

I remember leaving for Texas to film *The Alamo* and being there for four months. My prince called me every night.

What in the world made me think that talking to someone for four months on the phone would give me a true picture of the man?

It takes living together, experiencing each other, making sure you fit emotionally and physically. Having the quarrels, making up, and experiencing together all that life entails.

But oh no, I was so smart. As it turns out, I was crazy, to get married so fast without really knowing him.

I got a letter from Cary years later; he was in Europe. It was a short note saying, "Where are you, Linda?"

I remember that when I read that letter I felt as if an elephant had stepped on my heart, but I didn't know why. Something was vitally wrong and I knew what it was.

I had been a coward.

Dear friends, don't be afraid of love—even if it costs you tears, it will also give you laughter. But most important, you will be alive and happy, because you will have lived.

I wrote back to him that I had married and I had two beautiful boys. I described a little about my husband, Yale.

The next letter from Cary said, "Congratulations. I am so happy for you and your husband and I wish you both all the very best for the rest of your lives."

Somehow that lit the fuse, which would take six years to reach a mountain of dynamite that would blow high, painfully, for the rest of my life.

My dear reader, these are some of salty tears I promised in this book.

Chapter 12

MEGATON HARRY

After *The Perfect Furlough,* I contemplated the panorama in front of me. I expected the studio would be looking for scripts for me; instead, they were lending me to United Artists, making money on me, to make a B movie called "Cry Tough" with an inferior actor, Johnny Saxon.

I laughed very loudly when United Artists realized what they had in their hands. Linda Cristal was a goldmine. My figure, wearing a short, silky slip, occupied 95 percent of the movie posters; down to the left there was a little drawing of Johnny Saxon, their starlet.

I said, "Ha…Eat your heart out, Universal. I don't need you."

Soon thereafter, my agent told me about an independent movie being produced privately, called *Love and the Midnight Auto Supply,* starring Michael Parks.

I was anxious to get going again and Michael Parks was an acceptable actor. Since the script was still in the process of being written and time was of the essence, they would shoot first the last scene of the movie.

I heard that they had called a famous stunt genius nicknamed "Megaton Harry", who was always very busy and worked for all the studios.

At the makeup table, Buddy Westmore, my makeup man, said, "This is going to be exciting. I hear that he is fantastic."

I answered, with a little giggle, "I hope you're right."

So I reclined myself in the chair, stretched my legs out, and prepared to wait. One hour went by… then two.…

Finally, the assistant director called, "Linda…Michael…we are ready."

We went to the entrance of the stage, and the "genius" came out. The man was missing his left arm and his right leg, walking with crutches toward me.

When I saw him, I gulped and swallowed, trying to smile.

After saying hello, he said, "This has to be a one-shot take. So I will be very precise. I will remain outside and use a megaphone. When you hear me say one, you will walk to this position. When I say two, you will walk sideways to this other position. When I say three, run out like hell."

I was excited. We assumed our positions. I heard him say "ONE," and all of a sudden all kinds of projectiles flew all around me—in front of my face, to the sides, above my head. I didn't wait for two and three—I flew out like a cannonball. I heard, "Cut!"

My heart was beating so fast, I thought I would never take another breath again. The genius said, "Perfect, good-bye" and quickly hobbled off.

Dear readers, that day I learned that there are two kinds of challenges: one for intelligent people, the other for morons.

My last challenge had almost killed me; I needed to be sure my future ones didn't. So perhaps riding an untamed stallion with no saddle on a beach in Australia was not one of my more intelligent decisions.

Chapter 13

AUSTRALIA

My agent got a call for me to film a commercial in Australia for Lux soap, one of the leading facial soap companies.

Australia? I said to myself. *What do I know about Australia?* I looked into it and found an article that said that the large, beautiful commonwealth of Australia is surrounded by 300 islands in archipelagos.

It was like going to another planet!

I wondered why Lux soap would go so far just to shoot a commercial, when we could have gone to Catalina or even Hawaii. But they had the money, and they wanted something unique.

After the long flight, I was jet-lagged. Gene, the lady who had helped me dress at Universal, flew in with me. She and I had become friends.

The next morning, she came in with something in her hands. "Here is your costume, dear."

I looked at the thing she was holding in her hand and could see her, right through it on the other side. I shook my head.

"I don't blame you," Gene said, "for not wanting to wear it. But I'm sorry, you have to put it on."

I put it on, and I was basically nude. But I wasn't going to give up.

I never saw a more beautiful beach anywhere in my entire life. Miles and miles of pink sand surrounded us, with some elevations that could be called mountains.

Shortly after I arrived, I heard a voice from a megaphone: "Linda."

I said, "Yes?"

"Take the megaphone from Gene's hand and talk to me."

I took the megaphone and said into it, "Okay."

"They are going to bring a white horse for you—very tame, so don't be concerned."

I said, "Okay."

"Get on it and, after you feel comfortable, kick him in the ribs to make him go into the water."

I said, "But there is no saddle on it."

"I know, a young man will help you get on it. When he's gone, just touch his right side and the horse will go right in the water."

A boy of about ten or twelve appeared and asked me in a low tone, "Are you sure you want to do this?"

I said, "Yes, there is no problem, right? He is tamed?"

The boy giggled and said, "Up to you," and helped me up.

I heard somewhere in the distance, "Action!"

The horse and I began to walk through the dry sand. He was gentle. I heard, "Cut! Very good, Linda. Another take."

I did as asked.

"Now, touch him again and pull his mane to the right, and he will go into the water."

I did that and the horse began to buck violently, as if a bee had bitten him. I knew I had to take a fall or I would be a goner.

When the horse turned away toward the water, I jumped off to the left, but instead of fluffy sand I hit the hard sand and the damn horse kicked me in the ribs.

I heard screams from the crew, and soon, an ambulance siren. The pain was so intense; I couldn't breathe. I couldn't hear the horse, and I hoped he was gone.

I must have fainted, because when I opened my eyes I was sitting on a canvas chair with my arms crossed around my ribs, saying, "I…am…going…ouch…to…sue…the…hell out of them!"

Gene said to me, "No…don't do that. Don't burn your bridges. How do you know they won't give you another commercial someday?"

"I wouldn't do it for ten million dollars."

They had given me a sedative for the pain and I went to sleep. I began dreaming. I had kidnapped the executive president of Lux soap and carried him in my own personal helicopter, which I piloted myself, to an area infested with sharks. I dropped him in the middle of the water and flew back, watching the giant sharks licking their chops.

When I woke up the next morning, I had a smile on my face.

Chapter 14

EGYPT

At an Oscars dinner party, I met a man named Italo Zingarelli. He told me, "I am going back to Italy tomorrow and I have an idea I want to propose to you. I want to produce a second *Cleopatra*."

I said with a giggle in my voice, "They are already doing *Cleopatra*—with Elizabeth Taylor, no less."

He responded, "She is going to give them a lot of trouble filming it. Would you be willing to forgo your salary and go on a venture of a second *Cleopatra* with me?"

My answer was, "When is the next flight out?"

That evening, I was so excited I couldn't sleep. I tossed and turned all night, to no avail.

Finally, I sat up and walked to my home theater in the back of the house, and picked up one of my photo albums. At random, I opened the page and there I was with Elizabeth Taylor, sitting four seats to my left, looking at me with fury in her eyes. Behind her was her Italian husband, trying to catch me with his wandering eye.

Smiling with a giggle, I sat on the arm of the recliner. As it happened, the public didn't yet know that yes, Elizabeth Taylor was a beauty from the waist up, but from the waist down, she had short legs and was just five-foot-four.

After landing in Rome, Italo said we had a second flight to catch in an hour. "Let's have dinner."

I said, "I think I have had enough flying for one day."

He said, "No, no, there is another connecting flight, we have to catch that flight, we have no time to waste.

"We are going to Egypt... ."

I almost screamed, "EGYPT?!"

He said, "You'll love it. We will stay at the Hilton and you will see the most beautiful moon over the river Nile."

I giggled, and thought to myself, *This promises to be a unique adventure, and I will love it.*

When I woke up in the morning, I remembered our conversation the night before and ran to the balcony, excited to see the beautiful Nile, only to find a row of Egyptians: one urinating in the Nile, next to him a woman washing her laundry, and after that one facing me squatting and going number two.

My jaw dropped; I couldn't believe it. Was this the romantic Nile Italo was talking about?

Standing on the balcony, I stretched my arms, yawning, and took a deep breath, realizing the air did not have the promised aroma Italo described.

The phone rang; it was the head of Universal Studios, reminding me that I was still under contract to them.

I replied, "It appears to me that I am breaking my contract because obviously you have forgotten that I exist."

"We have not!"

"No? Then, why are you making a film called *Last Summer* with Rock Hudson and Gina Lollobrigida?"

"Linda, this is nonsense. We have great prospects for you. We have invested a fortune on you through the years. We have given you a career!"

I replied, "Yes, and it is not without some regret, but I must maintain my decision. Perhaps you forgot that actors are not only a piece of merchandise, but also a human being."

Chapter 15

THE SCORPION

Italians have a way of making the impossible possible. Suddenly, I was surrounded by designers drawing my figure, dressed as Cleopatra. There were also hairdressers showing crowns and wigs that Cleopatra wore.

Finally, there was a carpenter with a saw, cutting a long plank of wood that he said was for me to recline on.

I asked, "Why can't I just sit on my chair?"

He said, "You won't be able to. Cleopatra wore very tight garments."

So I leaned back and it was actually very relaxing. I could have fallen asleep on it.

The first day of shooting was next to the pyramids. Italo was trying to place the cameras in a way that would not show the hot dog and refreshment venders that tried to profit from the tourists.

I was supposed to be lying down next to a camel, who didn't seem to be happy with his position and looked at me with hate. He turned his head, facing me, chewing something.

They had bandaged my feet so they wouldn't burn from the hot sand, but of course we couldn't show that in the film. When I was in position, they removed the bandages.

I was lying down next to the camel and the director said, "Whatever happens, don't move. This is a long shot, so don't look for the camera, it will be focused on your face. Remember, you are asleep."

I held the position, which was not very comfortable—it was like lying on a frying pan.

After a few seconds, I peeked out from the corner of my eye. There was a little movement on the sand. Something was underneath it. It was coming toward me like a submarine, with a little periscope. It continued crawling closer and closer to me.

I began to get nervous. But I didn't dare move because it would ruin the whole shot.

Then, I realized it was a huge scorpion. I bit the inside of my lip, so as not to scream. The thing kept crawling…and crawling…and crawling toward me.

Finally, I heard, "Cut… Print."

I gave the longest scream ever. "Pick me up…pick me up! Don't ask questions, pick me up and run."

They ran over to get me, just before the scorpion got close enough to sting me.

Chapter 16

THE CHARIOT

Dear Reader, as I have mentioned several times, my life has always been one of challenges, thank God, and my desire to pursue them.

Here was a biggie.

In several of the scenes, I had to drive a chariot. Now, filming in the US, it would not have been possible, as they would have demanded a stunt woman do it; however, we were in Egypt, with a Italian crew that followed the order of the director without question. This promised to be fascinating.

They brought the chariot, being pulled by sixteen horses.

Dear reader, when seeing a chariot, led by not one but sixteen horses, some people would normally be apprehensive, if not terrified, but that's not me.

Stupidly thinking that the sixteen white horses were trained, I took the reins and, before thinking twice, I lifted my hands—and before I could give them a command, they took off.

My stomach went back into my ribs, but then I double-twisted my hands in the reins and, pressing my thighs against the front of the chariot for support, I said, *I can do this, I can do anything. Come on, let's go.*

Dear reader, two things come to mind. First, I guess I didn't learn my lessons regarding wild white horses from my experiences in Australia, Second, I should have asked the crew what was the best way to stop, or at least slow down, sixteen horses at once.

I figure out the answer on my own: they will slow down when they get tired.

Later, during filming, I recall that they sat me in a chair under an umbrella, and brought me ice water, which they placed on my neck and behind my knees.

While they were arranging the next shot, a little local Egyptian boy approached me. I was surprised that he spoke English.

He said, sitting at my feet, "Did you know you could fry an egg in the sand?"

I looked at him. He was cute, must have been six or seven years old. I responded, "That is very funny."

He said, "No, no…it's true. I could show you, if you give me an egg."

So, I called the cook in the company and they brought me an egg. The boy promptly cracked the egg in the sand next to me, and sat down to wait.

I looked at the egg in disbelief, but the yolk began to first get creamy, and then yellow, and then the white formed an aura around it—at which point the boy picked it up and swallowed it, as if he hadn't eaten in a while.

I began to laugh and laugh and laugh, and he said, "Missy…missy…can I have another egg?"

I said, "Every day that we shoot here, you come here and I will give you an egg."

Chapter 17

GEORGE KAUFMAN

Zingarelli explained to me the kind of Cleopatra he wanted to make. It would be a teenager Cleopatra, full of beauty and joy.

So, he brought me a belly dancer. The first thing the woman did was insert a fake ruby in my belly button (which eventually had to be removed surgically).

Belly dancing was definitely not rock 'n' roll. I thought to myself, *It's like Chinese torture.* My shoulders and hips had to make crazy motions I had never done before.

At night, I bit my lower lip, so as not to scream in when I had to switch positions in bed. I said to myself, sniffling, *Well, if the picture doesn't make it, I can always open a belly dancing school.*

But the picture not only made it, it flew to the ears of Lew Wasserman—via Louella Parsons, the number one reporter to the Hollywood stars, who had said, when I arrived in Hollywood, "Watch Linda Cristal—this young lady is going places."

There were a few days of celebration at the Hilton. We had champagne, caviar, dancing in the terrace—and, for me, the personal pleasure of beating Elizabeth Taylor again.

You see, readers, Elizabeth Taylor was going out with a successful businessman named George Kaufman, who, after sitting next to me at a group dinner at Spago in Beverly Hills, quickly dropped her and started dating me.

Lew Wasserman bought the film for one million dollars and George and I both had little bells ringing in our hearts, imagining our arrival to the opening of the film in Hollywood.

But it never opened. It never showed, because after seeing it, the studio realized that their $30 million dollar production with Elizabeth Taylor would never make it against the beauty of Linda Cristal.

Ahh…but destiny had a card up its sleeve…

Chapter 18

JOHN WAYNE

Back in Hollywood, I concentrated on my career. Where was I going from here? I read *The Hollywood Reporter* every day, looking for the answer. It had to be somewhere.

My agent invited me to El Morocco. It was a nightclub of fame on Sunset Boulevard—with Elvis Presley, no less. There was a red carpet extending from the sidewalk all the way to the stage of the club.

I walked in, looking at the stage. The room was zooming with excitement. Elvis Presley was king then.

My attention was called to a table on the right, a group of people laughing and drinking with joy. A strong arm grabbed my arm, my body twisted, and I fell onto the lap of someone who was completely drunk.

He said, "Ahh…look at what Heaven has sent me."

I took a good look at his face and recognized it was John Wayne.

He continued, "I know you…you are Linda Cristal, the Latin beauty." He was even drunker than I'd thought.

"Listen, Linda, I am going to make the biggest film ever produced in Hollywood, called *The Alamo.…*"

I thought to myself, *Yeah, right.*

He continued, "And when I do, you will be co-starring with me." He shook his head up and down, very intoxicated. "I have rented a town—Brackettville, Texas."

I answered, "Oh yes, of course you rented a town. You should drink less. Good night."

Four months later, the phone rang and a voice said, "Linda?"

I said, "Yes?"

"This is John Wayne. Are you ready for Brackettville?"

Dear readers, have you ever seen a picture of me looking stupefied? Well, you could have taken one now.

Life as a cowboy in Texas was a new page in my life. I wore blue jeans, boots, a cowboy hat—or should I say cowgirl?

I was the only female star in the ambitious film. I learned to shoot pool by joining the crew in the evenings. Sometimes, we used our payday cash to shoot craps; soon I was as good as any of the guys.

The days I didn't have a work call next morning, I returned to the big old Brackettville house that was allotted to me. There was a library on the first floor and an old comfy wing chair, where I made myself comfortable with a Sherlock Holmes mystery next to the fireplace.

I put my feet up, in case some uninvited crawling thing paid me a visit. I had never forgotten about the old man and the tarantula under the rock, or the scorpion with the periscope in the Sahara desert.

Shooting continued and I noticed that Duke (John Wayne's nickname) began to take longer and longer in setting his cameras for each shot. The production budget began to get shaky and I noticed the crew were murmuring amongst themselves and watching John.

One morning, a tall man wearing a black patch on one eye entered the set. He held the tip of a gray handkerchief that had obviously once been white, and, crossing his arms on his chest, watched Wayne. Someone next to me said, "Uh-oh, here comes Papa."

All this was fascinating to me. What were they talking about?

Something told the man that I was staring at him, because he suddenly turned and looked at me. I looked back and smiled. He approached me and, without saying a word, used the disgusting handkerchief to dry invisible perspiration from my forehead.

Since I didn't know who he was, I wanted to slap the handkerchief off of my face, but then he spoke.

"Are you a Latina? Well…we could debate about that. I am Italian, French, born in Argentina, and very curious to know who you are."

Without waiting for a reply, he put his hand under my chin and said, "Come and face the light."

I followed him with curiosity. He began to rearrange my hair, lift my chin up. He looked at one profile and then the other, and then said, "Yes…yes… Quite a beauty. I tell you what…would you like to make a film for me?"

Dear readers…this doesn't usually happen twice in one lifetime. The man, I found out, was John Ford. John Ford and Frank Capra were the same caliber of talent, and I was the luckiest girl in the world. Don't go away, more to come.

Chapter 19

JOHN FORD

The film continued, week after week. John Wayne made a habit of consulting with Ford on every shot. Stress and depression were taking over him.

He sent for an English actor, who came from Europe to play a Texan general. I thought this was a situation well worth watching closely—it could never work. How could an actor with an English accent play a Texan?

Twenty-four hours later, Laurence Harvey arrived, sounding like Cary Grant and carrying a goblet of red wine.

After saying hello to Papa, he smiled at me and, noticing my eyes were on his goblet, said, "I am always 'thirsty.'"

We all accepted his remark, without wanting to add more worry on Wayne's plate—it was already too full.

The shooting of *The Alamo* was an economic disaster.

My character only appeared in the first two hours of this 4.5 hour epic feature; Ford insisted on directing all my scenes.

Wanting to show my gratitude, once in a while I walked over to him and, picking up the end of the filthy gray hanky, I dried the invisible perspiration on my chin—he loved that.

Even though no one had ever seen John Ford smile, he smiled at me. Then turned me around, patted me on the backside as if I was a little naughty girl, and sent me on my way.

I left Brackettville and I heard the film went down royally, like the *Titanic.*

One of its important passengers was the nominated song for *The Alamo:* "The Green Leaves of Summer," written by Dimitri Tiomkin. It lost against a popular song of the times called "High Hopes."

But guess what? Would you believe that one day the phone rang and John Ford was on the other side saying, with a very strong Irish accent, "My darling little girl, would you like to go back to Brackettville?"

I wanted to scream no, but I held my breath.

"I am going to make a film called *The Last of the Fast Guns,* with Jimmy Stewart, Richard Widmark, and you."

I exhaled and, saluting like I was in the Army, I said, "Yes, sir." Then I hung up and, leaning back on my bed with my arms stretched, I exhaled.

Dear readers, remind me to tell you about my friend the skunk.

The thing that had me paralyzed with joy and fear was that I was going to be working with three multiple-Oscar winners: John Ford, Jimmy Stewart, and Richard Widmark.

Chapter 20

JIMMY STEWART

I arrived at the tiny Brackettville airport, exhausted. It was exactly midnight—the witching hour.

A black limo stopped next to the plane and the chauffeur removed his cap and opened the door for me. Cushioned comfortably in the soft dark seat, I fell asleep.

I have no idea how long we traveled. Finally, the car stopped in front of an old house and the chauffeur opened the door to let me out, brought in my luggage, and said good night.

All I remember now is that I saw a white pillow on a comfy bed, and I embraced it with immense gratefulness. Even though I was exhausted, I felt something crawling up my nose. I tried to shoo it away, but it was persistent. I tried again, to no avail.

Finally, I opened my eyes, inhaled deeply, and realized the house was on fire! Somehow I grew wheels under my heels and flew out the door screaming "Help…help…fire…fire…"

A tall man stood before me and held me in place, holding down my arms and saying, "Hold tight. I don't see any fires."

I looked up. I was facing Jimmy Stewart, and with a big smile that threatened to become laughter, he said, "There's no fire—it's probably just a skunk!"

Because the oder was so strong, It must have numbed my senses and I thought it was a fire.

He said, "You are very fortunate he didn't think you were a fire hydrant."

I remember, decades later, doing my daily exercise routine of jogging in Beverly Hills, I went by the corner of Roxbury and Elevado, where Jimmy Stewart's house used to be.

But it was there no more. Gone with the wind… Jimmy's "Blue Heaven," as he used to call it.

Something in my chest wanted to be heard and finally it broke loose in the form of a tear that ran down my cheek, kissing my lips.

People walking by, looking at me with curiosity. I reached for my dark glasses and, wiping off the tears, broke into a run.

Yes…sometimes this is a damn sad world. But on with the story…

Two Rode Together was shot using portions of the stages from *The Alamo*—thus saving money. My character was a white girl that had been captured by an Indian chief and saved by Jimmy Stewart.

Ford must have seen something in me that triggered his well known desire to help real talent, because he paired me with Jimmy Stewart and Richard Widmark. And if Ford believed in me, I figured, why shouldn't I.

On location, I was called to wardrobe, which was made of a huge canvas tent, where seamstresses were sewing and others were running around with drawing boards. These seemed to me to be like bees zooming around and I hoped they knew what they were doing.

The first scene showed me as a Native American girl, with a stripe of paint on my forehead. The next, wearing a beautiful long gown, my hair braided on top of my head like a crown.

I was a little perplexed when John Ford walked in with a script in his hand, his well known filthy handkerchief hanging from his mouth.

"Linda, I underlined what I am filming tomorrow morning, it is the ending of the movie. You will be in a carriage and will be saying good-bye to the love of your life, you're holding back tears of joy.

"Just look into the camera, and I will come in very close. Remember, the camera will see everything, I want those tears just barely starting to shine in your eyes. I want to do it in one shot."

Swallowing hard, I closed my eyes for a moment in preparation and thought, *The winged imagination of an actor is able to encapsulate a moment in time in the beat of a heart.*

Jimmy was sitting on top of the Western-style carriage, saying to me, "Okay, señorita, here we go...." His eyes were full of a promise of never-ending love.

While trying to work up the tears that needed to be real, and being unable to, I brought to my mind the image of my mother and father and how much I loved them. I thought about how I wouldn't be able to see them again and the tears began to fall.

Looking up at Jimmy, suddenly I was his wife, Gloria.

I heard Ford murmur "Action." I looked at Jimmy and, with tears running down my cheek, I thought, *Yes...*

Life during the filming of *Two Rode Together* was a ball of cherries. Jimmy was the most fabulous man I have ever met. He used to tell me about his wife—he called her "my blue heaven."

One day, while sitting on our canvas chairs, I asked him, "Why do you call her your blue heaven?" He turned to me and said, "Because going home to her is like going to paradise."

I thought, *There will never be another Jimmy Stewart.*

Chapter 21

RICHARD WIDMARK

Richard Widmark was the opposite of Jimmy Stewart, taciturn and introverted. Definitely a strange man.

We were shooting publicity shots for *Two Rode Together* in the gallery, when Widmark walked in. I was wearing a revealing bikini, a cowboy hat on my head, and short boots. Across my face, my best c'mon smile.

When Widmark saw this, he turned around and walked out, shutting the door with a big slam.

While the crew was arranging the lights for the next shot, I thought, *This man seems to have a chip on his shoulder, and it's against me.*

I noticed that if I approached an area where Widmark was running lines with Stewart, he would leave. If I came in with my lunch tray at the improvised commissary, he would pick up his tray, get up, and walk out.

In one scene, I was on my knees in front of Jimmy, kissing his hands in gratefulness for his having rescued me from the Native Americans that had captured me earlier. After I had finished, I lifted my eyes and saw Widmark staring at me.

I saw a mixture of emotion in his eyes. Hate? Admiration?

Dear readers…have I told you before that men are 99 percent difficult to read? So why try? Love them, and if you don't like it, leave them. But make sure that you're having fun!

After the movie was completed, I returned to Hollywood. I took an apartment on Sunset Boulevard. It was convenient, and close to a spot where people in the film world had breakfast.

Reading *The Hollywood Reporter* one morning, while I was having breakfast, I read about a TV series being shot called *The High Chaparral.*

I called my agent, who answered on the first ring. "Leon…here is a show that would be perfect for me. It's called *The High Chaparral.* It is the story of a strong willed young latin beauty."

He said, interrupting me, "I know all about it. Unfortunately, we are late. They already shot half the pilot with an actress by the name of Anne Caulfield."

"That's no problem," I said. "Just get me the interview, I'll do the rest."

"But Linda…" he said.

And I interrupted, "Listen—you do your job, I'll do mine."

When we arrived at the studio, we went straight to the producer's office. The secretary said, "Mr. Dortort is in conference with the studio executives."

I looked at my agent, and said, "Watch and learn."

Before the secretary could stop me, I walked into Dortort's office, closing the door behind me. I could hear the secretary in the background screaming, "Just a moment…just a moment!"

I never lacked guts, but I must confess that the oval table surrounded by twelve men in black suits and ties shook me a little. But what the heck—I was in the ring and I was going to fight the bull.

They all looked at me with curiosity. The one sitting at the head of the table said, "This is a private meeting, miss, can we help you?" He didn't even stand up to talk to me.

"No, you can not help me, but I can help you."

He stood up. "I beg your pardon?"

"My name is Linda Cristal and I am here to stop you from making a big fiasco. The best thing you can do is pick up that phone and stop your production."

He frowned and squinted, trying to make sense of me. Then he half-laughed. "Okay," he said, "this is funny." The rest of the black suits turned their chairs to face me.

"Okay," I said, "this is the deal. You're making a series about Latin people with an American lead named Ann Caulfield. Can you see where you are going wrong?"

As nobody spoke up, I continued, "Get rid of her and reshoot the pilot."

Now they all were laughing. One of the executives said, "This has to be a joke, David, one of your friends is pulling your leg."

I said, "Not at all. Let me show you what I mean. First of all, Anne Caulfield has no idea about the difference between acting and being."

They began to open their mouths to talk but I didn't allow them. I said, "Shh, listen to me. I will go one by one with each of you and I will show you what reality is."

I went to the first black suit and sat on his lap. Crossing my legs, I put my arms around his neck, and before he could react I gave him a kiss smack on the lips. It wasn't just one of those kisses that you do for television—this was the real McCoy.

He squirmed for a moment in his chair and then gave in and hugged me and then went to stand up—I almost fell on the floor.

"Did you notice the excitement of the kiss? Did you notice the reality of the emotion produced by the kiss before you reacted?" I asked. "I propose that if I am in the series, I will give you that excitement in every scene."

There was a long silence. I thought to myself, *Well…at least I gave them something to think about.*

Walking towards the door, I said, "I am going to give you five minutes to talk in private. After that, I am walking. If you're interested, I am outside with my agent and we can sign an agreement. If you're not interested, bye-bye—I am walking out and will be interested in seeing the reviews of your show."

My agent was outside, walking and pacing. There was a tall, slender young Latino man, probably waiting for an interview.

I sat down and stretched my legs out and said, "What's your name?"

He said, with a contagious smile, "Henry Darrow," and in a gallant gesture, he kissed my hand.

"Linda Cristal," I responded. "I suppose you're here for *The High Chaparral*?"

"Yes," he said.

"Do you like fireworks?" I asked him.

"Yes," he said.

I said, "Watch with me real fireworks, any moment now."

He sat next to me and we both stretched our legs and waited.

Within a few minutes, the door opened and David Dortort invited me in. Then he invited my agent in. The suits were gone.

"Sit down, please," he said. "As you know, I produce a show called *Bonanza,* but I want *High Chaparral* to be shot like a film, not a television show.

"By the way, I agree with you," he said, looking at me. "It is a show that should frame the Latin-American women of the early 1900s. We will think of a name for the character."

"I have a name for the character," I said. "My own."

"Linda Cristal?" he asked.

"No, I have another name, my middle name is Victoria."

"I am having my writers work twenty-four hours a day, because we have to rewrite the whole first half of the pilot and reshoot it. It will be an expensive proposition, but I have a feeling the studio will go for it. The executives seem to be impressed with you.

"How soon can you leave for Durango, Mexico?" he asked. "I want you to acclimate there yourself for a week or two while we work here."

Chapter 22

HENRY DARROW

When I arrived in Durango, Henry Darrow was already there. He asked me, "Do you ride horses?"

Readers…by now you know that I would say yes to any challenge. But after my experience in Australia, horses intimidated me. Regardless, I told him the truth: that I was not good on a horse, but had told the producers I loved them.

He laughed the most infectious laugh I have ever heard.

To make a long story short, we were put within a ring, with two horses waiting for us.

Henry asked, "Did they tell you that you have to ride both astride and side saddle?"

I said, "Well, I suppose if I wear pants, I ride like a man, and if in the next episode I am a woman, then…."

He interrupted, "Your left leg has to be laced around the horn of the saddle."

Thanks to Henry, filming the High Chaparral was the most fun I had in my life.

The High Chaparral was a huge hit and ran for five years, with me being the only actor on the show who won multiple golden Golden Globe awards, including Best Actress in a Dramatic Series.

Let me tell you about my character on the show, because dear reader, you're not going to believe this.

I believe someone up there in Heaven was looking down at me and smiling. Victoria had not only my name but also my temperament: my Scarlett O'Hara deviousness, my desire for challenges that brought fun into my life. She was who I really am.

Let me tell you about one of the scenes most loved by fans.

Manolito (Henry Darrow) is heading back from town, drunk with a bunch of ranch hands, singing a song about chickens. Victoria picks up a broom that was leaning on the front of the house and begins hitting them on the head in disgust.

Manolito covers his head, while he laughs and laughs and laughs, saying, "Hermanita… slow down, slow down. We weren't gallivanting this time, we were only drinking."

Victoria would not stop hitting them—*whammo, whammo.* Then, she noticed one of them was a very handsome young man.

Dear readers, in a million years I bet you could not guess who it was.

It was Clint Eastwood—the brilliant actor/producer/director and Oscar-winner. The one who made spaghetti westerns in Europe, his stepping stones to get back to Hollywood to be who he is today. If you don't believe me, I have photos of when he was just a pretty boy.

After *The High Chaparral,* I got a call regarding a new film to be shot with Charles Bronson called *Mr. Majestyk.*

That film was a struggle from day one. I think a sane actress wouldn't have even gone to test for the part. Here's why…

First of all, Charles Bronson would never play against any actress but Jill Ireland, his wife. Second, he had a reputation of being impossible to work with.

But, you know me. If I didn't get a taste of challenge for breakfast, I would feel I was starving!

One lovely spring morning, I woke up to the sun shining in my room. I stretched gratefully. My new agent, Leopold, called me, all excited. He was stuttering.

I answered, "Leopold, take a deep breath and relax. Nothing can be that bad. What is it?"

"Bad?" he replied. "Who said anything about bad? This is great news!"

I said, "Then tell me, you silly goose."

"Okay…the part of a melon picker in the south of Texas is up for grabs. You would be starring with the top box office money-maker in the country, Charles Bronson!"

Dear readers, I could write a whole book about Charlie, but first let me tell you how I got the part. It wasn't easy, but it was oh so much fun.

Leopold told me to dress in my finest. I decided to wear something modern, with a picture hat on my head that made me look like Scarlett O'Hara.

I looked fantastic. I watched myself in the mirror, lifting my chin up and pretending like I was talking to the producer, saying with pride, "Good morning…I am here to provide you with a test for the female playing with Charles Bronson in *Mr. Majestyk.*

"Yes, I said I am ready," I told the mirror.

The moment of truth was here. At the office, the secretary showed me in. Trailing behind me was the emotional Leopold.

Two men stood up to shake my hand and said, "Please sit down, Miss Cristal. How very nice of you to be interested in the part. Unfortunately, you're not at all the actress for it."

I looked at them interestingly and said, "I'm not? How do you know?"

Walter Mirisch, who was the producer of the film, was the first to speak. "Well, there's no doubt that you're a beautiful woman, but we are looking for a woman whose job is picking melons in the fields. All day in the sun."

Fleischer who was the director added, "She would be brown from the sun. Of course, that could be fixed with makeup, but you look so refined.…"

I replied, "Oh…of course, you're right. Now I understand that you wanted to see the character—I thought you wanted to see Linda Cristal. Don't worry, I will be back tomorrow, as the character."

With that, I walked out, with Leopold behind me.

When tomorrow arrived, I dressed in cowboy pants, boots, and a white shirt, open at the neck with the sleeves rolled up. On my head, I wore a cowboy hat.

As we walked into their office, I picked up a wooden chair and, placing it in front of their desk, I straddled it. With my right thumb, I lifted the hat and said, "Now, you two motherfuckers…am I the character or not?"

Chapter 23

CHARLES BRONSON

Entering the glass-enclosed VIP boarding area at the airport, I saw Charlie Bronson. He was strolling along, a hat that screamed "do not disturb" covering his face.

Although I had heard that he was not a friendly man, I smiled, thinking, *Oh well...people love to gossip, and when they run out of gossip they make things up.*

So I squared my shoulders and, approaching him, I said, "I know that we will meet tomorrow on set, but I thought it would be nice if we had a chance to say hello and get to know each other a little bit."

He cut in, "You thought?" and looked at me from under his hat. "Obviously, you don't have a brain that thinks, and I would appreciate it if we could try to ignore each other as much as possible."

The few people around us were staring at us, and my blood rushed to my cheeks like a swarm of angry bees.

From then on, it was war! We found ways of making each other's life impossible.

One morning, I went with the second unit to a vast remote corn field, where Charlie and I were suppose to escape from the bandits that had shot his watermelons.

On set, I had looked at the rigged truck, which was being worked on. One of the crew said, "Make sure you leave just enough gasoline for the stunt, we want to make sure it doesn't blow up when it hits the ground on the other side of the fence."

I thought, *Hmm. I know they are not planning to let me drive it myself, but I suppose everything is open for negotiation.*

I began to get excited. Something told me this was my day. I looked around and saw the makeup man stuffing some rubber boobs down the blouse of Crazo—the stunt man. They called him Crazo because he did the impossible stunts, the ones no one wanted to do.

When all was done and the crew was rehearsing the scene for the camera, I approached Crazo and, standing on my toes, I murmured something in his ear. He listened for a moment, and then turned his head abruptly toward me with an expression of alarm.

"Oh no!" he screamed. I quickly reached for his arm, pulling his ear down to my lips, and murmured something else.

He shook his head.

"Okay, suppose I add all my per diem, and give it to you."

He looked at me. "It isn't a matter of money."

"Come on, Crazo, everything in this world is a matter of money." Then I said, "Okay, I will give you a percentage of my salary for this movie if you let me…."

He looked at me and smiled. "You women…it's a deal."

The director of the second unit said, "Ready to go."

Charlie, who had been in his trailer, came out to do the scene. I noticed that Crazo was securing Charlie's legs to the back of the pickup. Charlie didn't even know I was there.

When the director said "Action," I ran from the opposite side, jumped into the driver's seat of the pickup, took the wheel, and, pressing the gas pedal to the ground, accelerated with the speed of a bullet. The truck jumped and was running on its back wheels. All I saw was corn ears flying by on both sides of my face.

In the radio in my ear, I heard Crazo say, "When I say 'ready,' pull the steering wheel toward you all the way and close your eyes."

So I did, and we flew over the fence, landing on the other side.

Oh God, I thought, *what a glorious day.* Looking up at Heaven, I said, *Thank you, Lord!*

Another scene involved Charlie holding a rifle in his hand, while kneeling on one knee. My hands were on his shoulders. Charlie was waiting to shoot the bandit who was stealing his watermelons.

Dear readers…I was carrying a huge chip on my shoulder against Charlie and I had prepared a goodie for him.

As the director said "Action," I dropped a drawing I had made of a woman sitting on her backside, legs bent at the knees, with her skirt pulled up to her chin. The sign said COME AND GET IT DADDY.

Charlie stood up abruptly, and I swear I could see the beginning of a smile!

That night, Fleischer asked me to dinner…. My instinct perked up its ears; was it dinner or something else?

Even before my hand reached for the menu, he grabbed it. Eyes full of emotion, I said to myself, *Oh no...*

He said, "Linda, you have to promise me you will stop provoking Charlie!"

I furrowed my brow. "Provoking?! Try humanizing! For God's sake! How do you expect me to play love scenes with an idiot?"

Fleishner replied, "No problem there. Charlie already tore all of the love scenes out of the script. Look, Linda, this is the first time Charlie has played in a movie with an actress other than his wife—he was forced to do it by a simple clause the Screen Actors Guild reminded him of. That word is 'discrimination.'

"You're a resourceful woman—find a way to finish this film. Charlie is the biggest box office money-maker in the industry right now. Deal?"

I thought for a moment, biting my lower lip. And answered, "Deal."

The corners of my lips lifted in a malicious smile, I thought, *This is not over yet. I am not finished with you, Charlie....*

Dear friends and readers, if I were a cat, you would see me swaying my tail back and forth, eyes closed and pretending to be asleep, going *purrrrrrr.*

No, I thought. *The film is not over and I refuse to give up. Charlie, you might be a big rat, but I am a wild cat.*

Dear readers, I promise you romance, laughter, one of my most challenging stunts ever. I am not going to tell you now, but will tell you later, I promise…

All things come to an end, and so did the movie. *Finally!* I thought. *Thank God! This chauvinistic Czechoslovakian-Lithuanian sack of shit will be out of my life forever!*

After Charlie's character won the battle against the bandits that had been shooting his precious watermelons, we came to the last scene of the film.

Fleischer explained that we were supposed to ride the jeep up the hill into the paradisiacal blue yonder.

The director had added, "You keep driving until I let you know by radio that you're out of sight and can stop. It has to be long enough for me to superimpose the final titles and the words 'the end.'"

When we got beyond the camera's vision, Charlie stopped the jeep and seemed to be thinking for a moment. Then, he slowly turned to look at me. I had never seen that look in his eyes before, so I furrowed my eyebrows and tried to read what might be going on in the prick's mind.

A few seconds went by. Suddenly, putting both hands on my shoulders, he turned me around so I was laying on my back over his knees, and, curling down to hold my face with both hands, gave me a kiss on the lips: tenderly, teasing, biting, licking.

When he was satiated, he lifted his head to look at my bewildered face.

I could only mutter, "Oh my! I just…but…didn't you say you hated me?"

He responded, "Yes, but I didn't say I didn't want you!"

We both broke out laughing.

The reviews from the Hollywood Reporter of *Mr. Majestyk* came out, saying:

"Linda Cristal is outstanding as an intelligent, beautiful farm worker organizer who falls in love with Bronson and stays with him despite mounting danger. Their man-and-woman-against-the-world relationship gives *Mr. Majestyk* unusual sweetness; Cristal plays no wimpy cliché; she's totally involved with the action, and an equal partner to Bronson's courageous stand."

Dear reader…little did I know that decades later in Beverly Hills, I would be coming out of an art gallery on Rodeo Drive—wearing an all-white white fox hat and a fox fur coat, and boots with high heels—when who would I run into but Charlie Bronson.

He said, "Oh Linda! What a surprise! You look like a snowflake. How about having dinner with me, for old times' sake?"

I replied, "Charlie…you are dangerous, unpredictable, and at times…delicious. However, I can't take a chance with you. What about if you swept me off my feet?"

We looked at each other and a little giggle escaped my throat and then his, and we both laughed, going into the restaurant next door, arm in arm.

Chapter 24

MY LAST CHANCE

All in all, what a wonderful life I have had. To say it had all the colors in the rainbow would not be true, because it would take ten rainbows. Such is the uniqueness of my life.

Dear readers, having read my vignettes, you have a unique knowledge of my life; however, there were many events I did not mention that were either "not completely legal" or public information.

For instance, my trip to the edge of our planet's atmosphere. Now, before you think I've lost it, let me explain.

While attending an Academy Awards event, I happened to sit next to a popular astronaut, who will go unnamed for now. I could tell he liked me, and he mentioned that he had seen my movies and heard that I like to take chances.

Then he added, "Could I offer you one?"

"One what?"

"A chance…actually, a chance of a lifetime. Let me explain. As you know, I am an astronaut, and have certain 'privileges' that are not discussed openly. One of which is the ability to take test flights to the edge of the atmosphere."

"Deal!"

Two days later, I found myself at a secret location adjacent to the LA airport. Moments later, I hear a distant sound that grew louder and louder.

As I looked up, I saw an aircraft approaching and then landing on the private runway in front of me.

Now, I call it an airplane, but it looked more like a small, single-passenger rocket. It was gray, with very small wings on each side. In fact, it looked like a bullet.

The astronaut got out, walked up to me, and said, "Ready?"

"As ready as I'll ever be…"

He got in first and then I sat in front of him—the space was tight for two. He then handed me a tube and said, "Put it in your mouth and breathe through it."

Moments later, I felt the nose of the bullet lifting, with me lying flat on my back. The sound of the bullet was getting louder and louder, and I felt my body compressed against his as we shot straight up.

I don't know how much time went by, but next thing I remember he was saying to me, "Here we are."

I opened my eyes and saw millions of stars. I said, "Oh…how beautiful."

Then he said, "Now we are going back." With that, the bullet turned over and we were upside-down. From there I had a view of the curvature of the Earth, and it was spectacular. I closed my eyes for a moment, thinking, *Maybe it's all a dream….* But it wasn't.

When we landed, he hugged me and said, "Remember, this is our little secret."

Dear reader, I can honestly tell you that this was the most exciting chance that I took in my life.

Thinking back, I am still amazed how a poor little girl from Argentina with just a few pennies, no parents, perseverance, and dreams was able to not only become a star, but to see the stars. Aren't you?

Printed in the United States
By Bookmasters